in PLAIN SIGHT

LEARN TO SEE WHAT MOST PEOPLE MISS
AND EMBRACE LIFE AS IT IS

BY
STEVE LENTINI

Edited by Digital Content
Creators – Jan Zucker

In Plain Sight: Learn to See What Most People Miss and Embrace Life as It Is

Copyright © 2024 by Steve Lentini

All rights reserved. No part of this publication may be reproduced, stored in a retrieval system, or transmitted in any form or by any means—electronic, mechanical, photocopy, recording, or other—without the prior written permission of the publisher.

ISBN: 979-8-9898956-0-1 (paperback)
ISBN: 979-8-9898956-2-5 (hardcover)
ISBN: 979-8-9898956-1-8 (ebook)

Library of Congress Control Number: TXu 2-408-763 Effective date 01/02/2024

Edited and Produced by Digital Content Creators - www.digitalcc.us

Cover design by Aaniyah Ahmed - www.99designs.com/profiles/1749467

in PLAIN SIGHT

LEARN TO SEE WHAT MOST PEOPLE MISS
AND EMBRACE LIFE AS IT IS

Acknowledgments

I have many people to thank for their wisdom during my life. Some of those are my family and extended family, Gifford Booth, Rich and Sue DiIorio, Kathyann, Thomas and Melissa, Christopher, Rob and Ashley, Jim Walker*, Jim Roche, John Donlon, Warren Gibbons, Paul Scoglio, Jack O'Keefe, John Brown, Mike Goddu, Gary Brustas, Peter Panagakos, Ross Kurz, Marc Borak, Marisa Chen, Jeff, "Z," and Walt, all of the Noonan crew, and so many more. Also, my children, Beth, Lisa, and Paul, and my grandchildren, Lacey, Lauren, Teagan, Logan, Miles, Taylor, Harper, and Griffin ☺, whom I love wholeheartedly.

Some of the wisdom you have all poured into me is shared here with the world. Thank you, and I am so grateful the Universe gifted you all to me.

Last but certainly not least, the Divine Creator of this miracle we live in. My blessings and gifts have been many, especially the most different moments and the places I fell short. They have been my most outstanding teachers and are part of embracing life as it is. They were gifts from the Divine as well. We are here to live life fully, not perfectly. Perhaps you think you are better than others or judge others who have fallen; that I suggest is what you are here to overcome.

*Jim Walker, rest in peace. He passed on May 12, 2023, while I was writing this book.

Prologue

What you are aware of, you are in control of; what you are not aware of is in control of you.

—**Anthony de Mello**

We miss so much in life; our hubris and ego blind us. We are blind to the gifts that life provides. Nature shows us how to live, which is but one of the gifts in this miracle. I hope you will see with this book that life ***is feedback.*** That is the gift.

One of my favorite quotes from Joe Dispenza is, "If we have strong beliefs about something, evidence to the contrary could be sitting right in front of us, but we may not see it because what we perceive is entirely different."

Humans gather evidence to prove that what they believe is true. The danger is that sometimes, it's just a story we tell ourselves. We want to be correct and miss what is in plain sight despite evidence to the contrary. It's called confirmation bias.

I will cover my mistakes when I can't see what is in plain sight. It's ego, anger, inner rage, wanting something different than what reached me, and all the moments I rejected that were gifts. I will share stories of friends, clients, and others who learned to "see" and their lives changed forever.

Ernest Holmes once said, "The illusion is how we look at things. We have looked at poverty, degradation, and misery until they have assumed gigantic proportions. We must look at harmony, happiness, plenty, prosperity, peace, and right action until they appear."

We miss what is in plain sight, which is that we live in a miracle, an infinite universe because we allow what we are unaware of to control us. The constant voice is continuously judging, deciding what is good or bad, and making others wrong so we can limit what is possible for our lives properly. Consider if your judgments hem you in.

Contents

1. Living a Life of Friction and Being Disturbed 1
2. The Cost of "Not Giving an Inch." 6
3. The Mirror Principle 9
4. The Waste Regrets Are. .13
5. Living in the Moment. .16
6. The Power of a Declaration 20
7. Taking a Stand 23
8. Entropy 29
9. Persistence. 31
10. Generosity of Time, Talent, Heart, and Spirit and the Impact of Its Opposite. 37
11. The Gift of Resistance and Difficulty 40
12. The Path Given 43
13. Waking Up to Life as Feedback 47
14. Eckhart Tolle's Ten Principles 50
15. Living with an Open Mind 52
16. We Shouldn't Call Death, Death 57
17. The Clues That Nature Provides. 68
18. Change Your State of Consciousness—The Law of Growth . . .75
19. Epilogue. 78

DISCOVER YOUR LIFE'S PURPOSE!

Feel Like Your Just Drifting?

This Short Quiz Will Unlock
Unlock the Clarity You've Been Seeking

INPLAINSIGHT.PRO/BONUS

1.
LIVING A LIFE OF FRICTION AND BEING DISTURBED

George Ivanovich Gurdjieff said, "Live a life of friction. Let yourself be disturbed as much as possible, but observe." My goal as a coach is to bother my clients as much as possible. As a result, I've led many to become more self-aware and observant. In my book *Wake up, Jump into Your Life*, and in my Zoom classes, I share how the principles of friction and disturbance assist in living a life of joy, satisfaction, and happiness. As we enter this new year, I want to take this opportunity to share how being at peace with these two principles can lead to a lifetime of prosperity and satisfaction.

The natural response to friction and disturbance is to surround oneself with like-minded individuals who support our beliefs and nurse our wounds. Many of us have successfully set up walls and safeguards to shut out the unwanted and, ultimately, unknowingly, ourselves. Attempting to avoid conflict, we've managed to circumvent self-observation. We can see all the escape routes in modern society as statistics show increased alcoholism, drug addiction, obesity, TV consumption, video games, and sex.

So, why friction? Society urges the opposite and encourages the avoidance of any upset or anyone who "rubs you the wrong way." Look at today's political scene, and you'll see how difficult it can be to get along, let alone begin to negotiate with differing views. But, despite the sometimes awkward tweets, this environment of friction is what we require to learn and grow. In her book *The Dark Side of the Light Chasers*, Debbie Ford said, "The people and situations that make us uncomfortable are mirroring back to us, the parts of ourselves that we have not acknowledged. What we don't know that we don't know." Therefore, self-observation and awareness begin by analyzing our daily situations and the interactions that have brought about friction in our thinking. Consider this path a journey, not a destination. You will never look back once you embark and see how your life changes.

"Embracing life with occasional friction and disturbance involves interacting with people or situations that make you uncomfortable, not eliminating or avoiding them." When faced with a discombobulating circumstance, I suggest seeking to understand with empathy, especially if you're feeling a profound internal disturbance. Take the opportunity for self-discovery into "What we don't know that we don't know" as Debbie Ford wrote in her book *The Dark Side of the Light Chasers.* We understand that resistance in physical exercise builds our endurance or muscles. Life is no different. Resistance in life is building our muscles for living. Typically, the more significant the goal or vision one has for one's life, the more resistance one experiences. It is life itself training and preparing us for our big goal. If we can make that slight shift (for some, it is a significant shift) and embrace resistance as necessary training, we can be excited that we're on the way toward our goal. More on this later in chapter 12.

Teaching myself and others to become self-aware involves questioning the source of friction or disturbance between people and events. Below, I've outlined a few questions that may assist you in better observing your thinking.

How has this specific situation made you feel? Why?

What is the perceived threat or hurt?

What are your similarities and specific differences?

Why is it that you've chosen to react?

Are you limiting your thinking?

By accepting an attitude of gratitude towards friction, which comes about despite any escape or resistance, we ultimately find happiness. I am still learning to overcome my "acorn brain" or the "little fucker" who often shouts into my consciousness, inviting me to make myself and others wrong. Rainer Maria Rilke called that voice "the little hooligan." Will I allow that little hooligan to run me, or will I run it? What will you choose? See the quote on the title page by Anthony de Mello. As Eckhart Tolle says, "Some people think that reality is nuts, and when you fight life, life fights you."

Only by inviting those who disturb me with open arms can I learn how small-minded I am in some areas of my life. Accepting all moments of my life as they show up, I surrender to what is and take it as part of the more fantastic plan. I can have a sense of humor about my acorn brain and overcome it by making a new choice to love and embrace the gift that friction brings.

The oyster yields a pearl only by living with and accommodating an irritating grain of sand.

Who are the grains of sand in your life? What events are the same?

Choose to make your life one of embracing friction and disturbances as the gifts you have not unwrapped. Accept them as a favor for turning you into a pearl over your lifetime, and in each moment, you might find the joy, satisfaction, and happiness you have been seeking through avoidance.

Wayne Dyer said, "When you squeeze an orange, you get orange juice; when we get squeezed, we get what we need to work on."

How can you overcome believing your thinking? Just observe what and or who triggers you. It might come as you start "self-observation." You might catch it during an outburst of depression or observing yourself linking outside events to your happiness. Nothing from the outside will "make you happy." Have you said, " I will be happy when this or this happens"? It's a question, not a statement. Self-observation is something you can discover on your own and experiment with, accepting your flaws as gifts and accepting all that comes as a gift.

Self-observation will initially lead to "the terror of the situation," as Gurdjieff called it, and, in my experience, an understanding of what was underneath it all.

Computers have apps we can click on, and underneath all the apps is the "program running all the programs." It's no coincidence that humans wrote programs that model how we live our lives.

Through self-observation, I've discovered that self-loathing was the program running all my "programs." Forgiving myself, flaws and all, and loving myself helped. It's a journey, not a destination. Some days are better than others, as the acorn brain works daily to remind me of all the places where I am less than or more than others.

You can prove the value of self-observation to yourself. Make it an experiment. The beauty of this is that there is nothing to do. Just notice what and who triggers you; over time, you will make new choices as you awaken. You will respond instead of reacting. I'd prefer to hyphenate "re-acting" because it reminds me that a reaction is from the past, a previously learned behavior that I am trapped by.

You will discover joy in running your life consciously instead of the mechanical responses the brain offers.

The brain has an advantage over us. It knows every mistake, humiliation, and error in judgment and reminds us at the most inopportune time. I can be driving down the road, and out of nowhere, my brain reminds me of the humiliation of peeing my pants in the first grade because I was too afraid and embarrassed to ask the teacher to go to the bathroom before our scheduled break. It picks different moments to remind me of the many places I have fallen or "re-acted."

I remind myself that all is a gift designed to help me make new choices. When I am aware of what hasn't served me, I can make a new choice. Consider this question: "What if nothing was personal and you *made* it so?"

Prove these ideas to yourself. Read *Self Observation* by Red Hawk or any of David R. Hawkins's works; if you want to dive more profoundly, read the works of George Ivanovich Gurdjieff or P. D. Ouspensky.

2.
THE COST OF "NOT GIVING AN INCH."

I think of this chapter and remember the times in New York City traffic when I would not give an inch to let in another car. I even risked damage to my vehicle. Others were doing the same, trying to get "one car length ahead." Once in Boston, a guy clipped my mirror as we both inched along, each of us sure we would "win." My ego resisted the idea of letting someone get ahead of me. My ego was driving me. *Am I losing anything by allowing someone space? Is this who I am deep down in life, not letting someone get ahead of me, even if it's risking damage? The Universe is spacious and infinite, limitless. Why am I so small-minded? Can I mirror this miracle I live in with unlimited thinking?*

Today, my goal is to be more accepting and spacious—like the Universe—in my thinking.

The gift in traffic is that I see the effect of a small-minded or limitless choice.

Which one brings more joy? When choosing either option, life provides feedback with the result. Who was upset? Who gave up joy in traffic?

The next question for me was, *Am I like this everywhere?* A coach once told me, "How you show up anywhere is how you show up everywhere." That is true, but it doesn't mean you cannot change. When you change, the same applies. Today, I shift in response to the feedback life provides. This awareness is a gift. "Imagine not knowing," I often ask myself and my clients.

Back to the earlier question, "Am I like this everywhere: Not willing to give an inch to allow others to get ahead of me, even risking damage?"

I didn't see it, and waking up to this behavior, once living in New York, I began to observe this part of my character. I had a competitive edge, and it was now blocking my joy. Part of it was positive, and the opposite, not so.

My job was to manage it now that I had become aware of the negative aspects.

Competition is healthy in a sport but not everywhere in life. Deepak Chopra suggests practicing "generosity of spirit" in life and that first, we need "simple awareness." I had become aware, and now I noticed that when I was generous, I felt more joy.

Test this idea and prove it to yourself. Like an experiment in science, notice where you are unwilling to give an inch and relax into what gives you more joy. Observe how you feel when you allow the car into traffic or give your time, talent, or wealth. What models this limitless Universe? The Universe continues its expansion, and at the same time, black holes are the Universe discarding the negative. Physicists may argue my theory, and metaphysicians might agree.

A model for living, expanding the positive, and discarding the negative?

Is this part of what we cannot see in plain sight?

Become aware of where you "re-act,"* and breathe, take a moment, and respond instead.

I said before that I prefer to hyphenate re-act because it's something from the past, something previously learned. There is no way to have a new future if we keep repeating history. Einstein said, "The definition of insanity is doing the same thing over and over again and expecting different results."

Joe Dispenza says:

> Psychologists tell us that by the time we're in our mid-30s, our identity or personality will be completely formed. This means that for those of us over 35, we have memorized a select set of behaviors, attitudes, beliefs, emotional reactions, habits, skills, associative memories, conditioned responses, and perceptions that are now subconsciously programmed within us. Those programs now run us because the body has become the mind. This means that we will think the same thoughts, feel the same feelings, react in identical ways, behave in the same manner, believe the same dogmas, and perceive reality in the same ways. About 95 percent of who we are by midlife is a series of subconscious programs that have become automatic—driving a car, brushing our teeth, over-eating when we're stressed, worrying about our future, judging our friends, complaining about our lives, blaming our parents, not believing in ourselves, and insisting on being chronically unhappy, to name a few.

Joe says, "If we have powerful beliefs about something, evidence to the contrary could be sitting right in front of us, but we may not see it because what we perceive is entirely different."

Ask yourself the following questions:

1. Has your body become your mind?
2. Is that small-minded, acorn brain running you?
3. Are you on auto-pilot, heading into a fog-covered mountain?
4. What are you missing in plain sight because of people or situations that bother you?
5. Are they a bother or the gift of life providing feedback about what to change?

3.
THE MIRROR PRINCIPLE

There are two aspects to the mirror principle. The first is "you must see value in yourself to add value to yourself," as John Maxwell says.

The second is a Rabbi Yisroel ben Eliezer, also known as the Baal Shem Tov, who elaborated on this point by saying, "Should you look upon your fellow man and see a blemish, it is your imperfection that you are encountering—you are being shown what it is that you must correct within yourself."

Until I was almost fifty years old, I spent much of my time seeing the "blemish" in others, and missing the gift of the mirror. The story I was telling myself was of a victim of circumstances, and I was the victim. I could see the imperfections of those around me and missed what was in plain sight. My imperfections!

That mirror reflected the anger of mates, anxiety, poor attitudes and work ethic, and leaders without morals or ethics. I was abused by a family member when I was eleven. My first experience of sex with others was oral sex from an adult. The mirror was complex to see what this experience showed me about myself. As an adult, I realized how manipulative a family member was, asking my twin brother and me to help him move. His goal was to have sex with us, and imagine asking us that at eleven. I could see that I was also manipulating others and how I came to learn that in our household, everything was swept under the rug. No one told the truth. I was child number six of seven and an identical twin. My twin was born four minutes later and, therefore, was the youngest. There was a large gap between us in age. When Stanley and I were born, Seb was nineteen, Lorraine was eighteen, Frank was sixteen, Bob was fourteen, and David was six.

Thirteen years after my father had passed, I discovered the reason for the age gaps. When I asked my mother about it, she said, "That was because your father was missing for five years." I was stunned. "Ma, how come no one ever talked about it or asked Dad, "Hey, pass the green beans, Dad, and where the fuck were you for those five years?" Mom replied, "I told the kids your Dad is coming home, and I don't want his time away ever mentioned." When I asked why, she said, "What good would it have done?"

When I asked my older siblings the same question, they all replied, "Mom told us never to mention it as what good would it do."

There it was. The reason I could always feel an underlying tension in the household. When we gathered for any reason, discussions at the dinner table were cordial and polite. How was your day? Or wasn't the weather fantastic today? We never learned to speak about what was happening or dared talk about the truth. My mother never told us about Dad and never made him wrong. She was right about that, and although we learned that from her, we also learned never to rock the boat.

I recognized all those traits in myself with the help of a coach. I gradually saw myself in the mirror as she asked, "What do your complaints about others tell you about yourself?" I was confronted and hurt by learning all this about myself and thought, *Imagine not knowing?* I began to see life as feedback, not as a story of defeat and victimhood.

I took an inventory of all my complaints about others. I looked at the list of each person and situation that bothered and upset me. Here is what the list looked like (I have changed the names to protect the innocent.):

Mary, angry

Tom, complains incessantly about his wife

Joe, a small-minded thinker

Sandy, anxious about life

Lola, a sex addict and cheater

Jim, a manipulative leader

Stew, unable to stand up for himself—people pleaser

My list was more extensive, and as I contemplated where I had these same character flaws over time, I discovered I did have them all.

As a result of this exercise: I began to work on each of them and to see that life was feedback. I was missing the gift of that feedback. Every step I took on this growth path yielded new results, such as more compassion for the people who bothered me; they were a part of the gift.

Joe Dispenza says, " Knowledge is power, but knowledge about yourself is self-empowerment."

Make your list of who and what bothers you; this list is your mirror. Begin the journey of self-empowerment. Take on each item on the list and be gentle with yourself about progress. For each item on my list, whenever I think I have conquered it, the Universe sends me a test. The Universe seems to have a sense of humor and responds, "So you think you have this down pat? Let's see." Think of growth as a journey, not a destination. Perfection is not the goal; progress is. Imagine *not* knowing.

Now, my calling is to speak the truth, no matter what. I call BSB. S. on my clients and can see what is in plain sight. I give feedback to others and risk their wrath. I have learned to invite and receive feedback because the option is to sweep it under the rug and then no one benefits, not me or my clients.

Brene Brown says in her book, *Dare to Lead,* "Clear is kind." When clients feel confronted by feedback, I say, "Imagine not knowing." The same thing I tell myself as I gracefully receive feedback. "Thank you for your feedback, and I will take that in and address it."

I suggest that you think about your response to the feedback. Do you defend and blame others? What is your automatic reaction? What is your perception of how others see you? What is their perception? Will you work to close the gap by inviting feedback?

Life is always for us, operating in plain sight. The Creator, the Creation, God, the Goddess, whatever you call the force that created this Universe, is walking beside you, never absent. When you can embrace life as it is, your life becomes the miracle that the Creator intended. The choice is always yours. Test this idea out; make your life an experiment. Please change what you put out and look for the gift. The other choice is to reject it all and complain. Which one sounds more fun?

4.
THE WASTE REGRETS ARE

"A life spent making mistakes is not only more honorable but more useful than a life spent doing nothing."

—George Bernard Shaw.

"The wise walk on clinging to nothing. They are neither elated by happiness nor cast down by seeming sorrows."

—The Dhammapada.

In his novel, *Time Is the Simplest Thing*, Clifford D. Simak wrote about space and time travelers who, when they traveled to the past, discovered no one else existed in the past, only they did at that moment. When you are in the past, only you are there. If it involves others, notice they have not joined you. We experience people who hurt us, and we hurt people. Considering that nothing is out of order in the Universe, how could it be so in our lives?

It is a romantic idea that our lives would be in perfect order only if things constantly matched the picture we have in mind.

If we can live in the moment, the past will reflect lessons learned because if we could change anything, we would not be in this place. You would not be reading this book, working where you work, or being surrounded by the people in your life right now.

What if everything in your past was perfect so you could be where you are now? If you are unhappy now, what if it's a key ingredient to your goal? Would you quit just before the finish line if you knew what your future holds? Regrets keep us stuck and prevent us from moving forward. The only value the past has is learning a lesson for our *future* and applying it in the now.

Gratitude and awe for living in the miracle are more accessible once you accept each moment as a gift. I propose that is what life is: a gift, feedback for learning, growing, and fulfilling your purpose.

This premise is what most people cannot accept. Embracing life as it is is a challenge. We are here to come to the point of embracing life with awe and gratitude, even for small moments each day. That is what most people miss, and it's in plain sight.

We would tell others what happened to us in the past rather than accept the event as guidance into a new future. You are fighting life when you resist what is happening; as Eckhart Tolle says, "When you fight life, life fights you" (*The Power of Now*).

Young people want to see many events from the past erased. I understand that. Presentism is the term. Imagine erasing all the painful historical events. what benefit would future generations gain from a "perfect past?" Progress in our lives and society comes from "touching the hot stove." The burns remind us to avoid that.

Regret is a gift urging us to forgive ourselves. What if you could say to yourself, "Well, it seemed like a good idea at the time," and laugh at yourself? The image of the laughing Buddha is of him doing that, laughing at himself. He collapsed under a tree from the burden of all his regrets and flaws. By studying with gurus and sages and reading everything he could find about living the perfect life, he convinced himself he would be the best Buddha. The burden of searching for that was his collapse. When he found humor in his flaws, he became the Buddha. Be gentle with yourself and learn to love yourself, flaws and all. Perhaps you could say that to yourself daily. I say it daily, many times over and over. It's working, as now I can laugh at what seemed like a good idea at the time.

When we can let go of our past and all the events in life that haven't met our expectations, we notice, at least in my experience, that we can be happy.

5.
Living in the Moment

"Life is a gift meant to be fully used before we leave the planet rather than squandered by living small. In short, don't return to your Maker less than fully 'used up.'"

—"Encouraging Words"

The Rev. Dr. Dennis Merritt Jones wrote the following in *Science of Mind* magazine,

> Do you put off doing what you are passionate about today because you are more focused on arriving at the finish line of life tomorrow rather than enjoying the journey along the way? Hunter S. Thompson had something to say about that mindset: "Life should not be a journey to the grave intending to arrive safely in a pretty and well-preserved body, but rather to skid in broadside in a cloud of smoke, thoroughly used up, totally worn out and loudly proclaiming Wow! What a ride!"

Reverend Jones continues,

> I love this quote because it reminds me that every moment of every day is a ride we paid for in advance—and our ticket

is good for today only. I don't know about you, but I have no intention of leaving this planet clutching an unused key. Metaphorically speaking, in what way might you be clinging a bit too tightly to the ticket for the ride of your life, waiting to use it until you have the time, an overabundance of resources, the courage, the permission or the---,---,:----(fill in the blank).

Living a life that allows us to fully use the gift of our physical, emotional, and material resources isn't a license to live stupidly. It's an invitation to live mindfully, with passion, optimism, and gratitude, remembering that the day that lies before us is really the only day we have to use our ticket because it expires at midnight every night.

What comes to mind when you read what the Reverend Jones says?

How thoroughly are you enjoying the ride? Are you? Does that voice in your head enroll you in everything that is not working out?

Fully living requires embracing the present moment, no matter what shows up.

At fifty years old, I had spent most of my life living in the past with regrets or in the future, frustrated if what I wanted wasn't as I had planned.

When I had my health challenge on November 13, 2002, I learned quickly to surrender to the moment and the value of surrender.

Your Calling—In Plain Sight

We all have a calling or a theme that life presents us with from all the events and people that show up. We miss what is in plain sight because we prefer the story, not the gift. We have a choice. We can see life as feedback and receive the gift or rail against it. The following chapters lay out my point. They describe amazing synchronicities that occurred for the people involved.

Waking people up to the gift of life as feedback started to knock on my door as a child. I had nightmares as a child that would take me out of bed and wander through the house. Mom would take me back to bed, still asleep. It took a force of will to wake up in those dreams. I recall that at the point of what seemed to be certain death, I would have to repeatedly declare, "This is a dream, and I am going to wake up." At age thirteen, I watched a daytime talk show featuring an expert on nightmares and how lucid dreaming could end them. I was glued to my seat as the guest said, "In the nightmare, you can jump into the dream, put up your hands and say stop."

That night, using the process he described, I did just that. The nightmares ended in my sleep world and had just begun in my waking world.

What followed was oral sex abuse by a relative, failed relationships, and business failures mixed in with happiness and success. I had stories to tell others about what was "happening to me" and missed the gift that life presented. It took that same force of will from my nightmares to see the gift life was trying to leave at my door. Life was knocking, and I hid, pretending no one was home. I was afraid to answer, and as I reflected, not ready anyway.

In November 2002, life kicked my door in, and I have been grateful for that moment every day since. My calling came crashing in. I had missed what was in plain sight, and it took nearly dying to wake me up. The gift was a peek at what was next. We hear the word death, which scares most of us; I know it did me until that day. I know there is a "next" moment in this infinite existence that mirrors what we live in, called a Universe, a mystery to all of us, even physicists.

What if we lived every day like there was always a "next" forever?

What if we lived without fear, thoroughly enjoying the ride?

What if "the good we do" is the only thing that matters to the Creator of the Universe?

What if our "mistakes or sins" are necessary for our growth?

What if our purpose is to overcome our small-minded thinking and to become more like the "superior reasoning power"* that created this miracle?*

What if everything and everyone who bothers us is a gift to wake us up? To help us grow and overcome our hubris.

John Maxwell says, "Our job is to get over ourselves in this life."

---

* As Einstein described, "The deeply emotional conviction of the presence of a superior reasoning power—which is revealed in the incomprehensible universe—forms my idea of God."

6.
THE POWER OF A DECLARATION

"We are called to be the architects of our future, not its victims."

– R. Buckminster Fuller

Declaring what we want or desire in this life is vital to manifesting that. Allowing yourself to think about what you want is the first step. Let me explain this with a story about a man I will call "J."

When I first met J, a client asked me to coach him. My client explained that J needed help with his goals. I met with J and asked him, "What would you like to earn next year?" I passed him a napkin from the restaurant we met at and said, "Write it down here and pass it to me." It took three or four times before he could admit he wanted to earn $100,000. His challenge was at his age; he was embarrassed to declare what seemed like a large amount of money for someone so young. He went on to earn more than that by double and more over the next few years.

I continued to coach J directly. Now he was my client. Fast-forward three years or so, we were sitting at a Starbucks beginning our coaching, and I got an overwhelming feeling he was holding something back, much like being unwilling to declare the $100,000 income goal. He was not allowing a desire to come forth. He did not "deserve" this in his mind. Feeling this firmly, I told J, "I am ending our coaching, J; you are holding something back from yourself and me. I will be glad to continue our coaching if you figure out what it is before our next appointment; if not, we are complete."

As I got up to leave, J said, "Sit down; I know what it is."

J said, "I want to be CEO of this company." There was something significant, a big goal, running around his mind, and he would not allow himself to believe it was possible and kept it a secret even from himself.

I sat down and said, "J, let's say 'this or something better,'" and explained that since his company had a CEO who was also the owner, his desire had to be general. I explained that since he did not own the company, he could still be the CEO someday, and if he added "this or something better," that allowed for additional options, and the Universe would do the rest. His job was not how it was to happen.

J now continued to think about his desire, picture it as instructed, and share it with people who would support his goal.

He had what I call "lessons" over the next few years as opportunities came from people who said, "I will make you a partner and CEO in the future." Those promises were empty except for the valuable experience he gained once he did become a CEO.

Life gave him the required learning to become what he pictured and allowed in his mind.

In the book *The Law of Attraction* by Esther and Jerry Hicks, Esther channels Abraham of the Bible, which is what Abraham says about manifesting what we desire. "Put your thoughts upon what you believe you want, and the *Law of Attraction* will draw more information, more data, and more circumstances to your creation."

J received all the above on his way to receiving what he wanted.

J allowed himself the grand vision, and it occurred. Abraham says this about "The Art of Allowing," "To be an *Allower* is to be one who feels positive emotion, which means that you must control what you are giving your attention to. It does not mean that you get everything in your world whipped into shape so that everything and everyone is the way you want it to be. It means that you are able to see, and therefore solicit forth from the Universe, from your world, and from your friends, that which is in harmony with you, while you let the other parts go unnoticed by you—therefore unattracted by you, and therefore not invited by you. That is *Allowing,* you see."

When J declared his desire to be a CEO, he *allowed that in himself.* He focused his thoughts and positive emotions on becoming a CEO because it aligned with his passion. Before his declaration, he struggled with what I call acorn brain thoughts like *Why would you be a CEO; you can never be a CEO; you don't deserve it, you don't have the education, and so on.*

Once he *allowed* that desire, it was like smashing a dam; what he experienced over the next few years was a flood of learning and experiences that did lead him to become a CEO.

The next chapter is partly about what J experienced and synchronicity. See for yourself.

7.
Taking a Stand

The following excerpt is from *Science of Mind* magazine, authored by Dr. Dennis Merritt Jones.

When was the last time you saw a dragon? Other than in a movie, you may say, never. Think again. We all have a few dragons in our lives. They come to us in many shapes and sizes. Some show up as our most challenging relationships. Others may reveal themselves through a physical or health challenge or our financial affairs. Irrespective of their origin, we would be wise to remember that we each have the power to tame the beast. But there is something we must do first.

The tendency is to withdraw, don our armor, and prepare for battle. There is abundant power in knowing that our greatest weapon of choice is our next thought. Will we react or respond to the intimidating roar of our dragon? Dragons don't scare easily, nor should they because they have something to tell us. Yes, dragons can talk. They are mystical messengers from a different realm of mind and don't reveal themselves to us to scare us but to get our attention to teach us something important if we will listen and learn.

The next time the dragon shows up as a challenge in some area of your life, rather than running from it or putting on your armor, consider standing your ground and asking it what message it brings. And then listen intently. You may learn exactly what you need to know to be the hero in the story of your own life.

The above fits perfectly into this chapter. I have a story about a man I call "Z." He is a loyal, hard-working man with principles he follows in life, and one is taking a stand. He changed jobs and discovered his new employers were not as conscientious. Suppliers were unpaid, and worse, payroll, including a few weeks of his own was frequently incorrect. His wife shared her concerns upon learning this, and Z decided to take a stand. Prepared to write a check for over $25,000 to pay suppliers and others, he went to the investor partner of the company. The stand was this; "this company needs new leadership, and if you want to keep me, I want you to make that change. I have just the guy to turn this company around. If you make this change, I have a check to help out because I cannot work where integrity is a second thought."

The investor made the change by hiring the man Z recommended as CEO (J in the previous chapter). The company made payroll, and the suppliers were paid, in part, with the check he wrote. What is fascinating is that the person who made the declaration in the previous chapter is the CEO who got the job. Synchronicity? Certainly!

Through this experience, Z found his life theme. Taking a stand is what he brings everywhere. It was in plain sight; after reflection, he could see all the times life called upon him to take a stand. He sees the results, too, of all the times he missed the gift. Every time he did take a stand, his life changed with fantastic effect.

Our calling is in plain sight, and many of us miss the opportunity life brings because we get stuck in the story. You might see the gift if you catch yourself wanting to be right instead of doing the right thing. Most of us want the story to complain to others about what or who has done us wrong.

Z could have stayed stuck in the complaint about the brothers who were mismanaging the company, and instead, he took action. After speaking with the investor about his complaints, he was willing to commit his own money to set things straight. He found his calling and can be counted on to this day to take a stand instead of complaining.

I took a stand once against the president of a company that I worked for in 2006 because he wanted us to break our word and not pay a client who had earned a rebate of more than $13,000, and I told him and my direct boss that it did not work for me to break our word. The president said, "But I did not give my word we would pay him." I replied, "Yes, but I did, and so did Cheri (my boss)." Effectively, he was saying that our integrity as a company was worth less than $13,000 because he was willing to break it for that amount. He asked me, "Why are you fighting for this client who left us." I said, "I'm fighting for our integrity, because we gave our word."

After six weeks of discussion, he agreed, and we paid the check. Although many people told me he had put a target on my back, I did not care because I have followed these principles. I have had many job offers, clients, and a steady income stream from multiple sources; not perfectly, mind you, but I fixed it when I realized something was out of whack with an apology, check, or whatever it took to make it right. Two years later, the company I stood up for and got the $13,000+ gave me a job offer that almost doubled my income from the previous job. What do you think they mentioned when we negotiated about the Director of Sales position? They immediately thanked me for standing up for them and said, "We know the kind of person you are and what you stand for . . . thank you for standing up for us." They also said, "We did not want you to risk your job for us." I said, "Don't worry, I didn't; I wouldn't work for a company that did not have integrity; if they had not paid the check, I would have left anyway."

Integrity does not mean you have to be perfect. Life is about learning from our mistakes. Clean up your mess once you realize you made it.

You have nothing to fear from anyone asking you to compromise your integrity. I ended up working for the company I stood up for, and I did not see that coming until it came, and I certainly did not see it in 2006 when I stood up for what was right.

Trust in the Law of Attraction, and you will see that you are always getting what you give.

Here's another story about a woman I will call "S."

One day I received a call from a former client who asked, "Steve, would you talk to one of my employees and tell me if I should fire her?"

I said, "No," you decide, and if you keep her, I will be glad to coach her if I accept her."

Twenty years later, she is a friend and one of my best clients.

Her strength is her willingness to take a stand and authenticity. She is willing to stand her ground and speak about what works for her or her role.

When she worked with people who could not see what was in plain sight, her role was to help them win. Once she became a leader, her speaking truth was sought out by her peers and bosses.

Today her path is leading teams, which has had many seemingly unnecessary stops. Looking back, she can see what she deemed as blocks or waste was the training she needed for each successive role.

Taking a stand as she is known for, and along with her authenticity, people know they can depend on S to do what is right.

What are you known for? What has been perceived by you as a mistake? Could it be that what you thought was a mistake was life guiding you? Christ said, "Everything works together for good." Mohammed said, "What has reached you was never meant to miss you, and what has missed you was never meant to reach you."

The shift in perception from life being a burden and a mess to embracing life as a fantastic gift that is always teaching us is amazing. You have to prove this idea to yourself. The Creator of a Universe or the Life Force, whatever you call it, is always present and always teaching. I don't need the Hubble or James Webb telescopes to tell me that. The images they send do remind me of it, though.

When you think in limits, you limit yourself and what is possible. Osho wrote the book, *Your Answers Questioned*, that title reminds me to stretch beyond limited, small-minded thinking and work to model the limitless, infinite thing we live in.

Work to stretch your limited thinking and consider life a gift and a guide. Whether you believe in the Divine or God, the Goddess, it doesn't matter. If you believe your thinking, that does matter. Humans think that we are on par with whatever created this Universe due to our ego, our hubris.

Consider what Einstein said when he was asked about his idea of God:

> I said before, the most beautiful and most profound religious emotion that we can experience is the sensation of the mystical. And this mysticality is the power of all true science. If there is any such concept as a God, it is a subtle spirit, not an image of a man, that so many have fixed in their minds. In essence, my religion consists of a humble admiration for this illimitable superior spirit that reveals itself in the slight details that we are able to perceive with our frail and feeble minds.

He also said, "Two things are infinite, the universe and human stupidity, and I'm not sure about the Universe."

After my near-death experience, I am sure about human stupidity, and I see more often today when that stupidity is attempting to run me.

Will you self-observe and receive the gifts that life is bringing you, or will you continue to be the victim, powerless and stuck with the stories you tell yourself about how your life just doesn't work?

In my experience, there is an intelligence infinitely larger than human thinking. We cannot see it because we think so small.

It's not my job to fix anything except myself in this world. If we all did that, the world would be a much better place, and I know it's all happening as it should for human growth.

8.
ENTROPY

Standing still in life is going backward, entropy. The Universe that surrounds the earth is still creating new stars and planets. While black holes have been discovered that suck everything in around them, to me, it signifies pruning or letting some things go while still creating anew.

> "Ludwig Boltzmann has shown that entropy exists because we describe the world in a blurred fashion." Carlo Rovelli
>
> *– The Order of Time*

So many of us want things always to stay the same. We do not wish to change. That may work for some, and it's entropy in action. Park a car in a field for a few years and watch what happens. Some people think that they will escape life unscathed by sitting still.

I suggest changing on purpose. I change things that I am comfortable with every year. It varies from who I work with to where I live. I have moved twenty-six times and probably have a few more to go, and I was seventy in 2022. I remember the English teacher told me at a young age, "You will never write a book." Now I have written nine, including this one.

If you feel stuck in a rut, life urges you to change and grow. Sometimes people who try to stay safe get a significant change delivered by life. Your changing proactively does not ensure that you won't get punched in the gut by life. If you learn to embrace it all as a gift, you will have a new way of responding to what occurs.

9.
Persistence

Many people quit just before the finish line. I know you have heard this before, but why? People often stop because of the acorn brain, that voice in their head says, "This is too hard; why do this? or Who you? You don't deserve this, or worse, and you are incapable; why did you believe you could?" Think "W Y D F L I" **W**hen **Y**ou **D**on't **F**eel **L**ike **I**t; do it anyway, *especially* then.

I had a coach who said, "Persist through the doubt." She was right! Challenges have shrunk every time, and I rose to the occasion by standing in doubt and persisting.

In high school, I tried out for football one day. I went with a neighbor and came home tired. The next day I was so sore that I didn't go. Later my neighbor told me, "Wow, it was an easy day today because the coach said we were probably sore."

For a few days, I regretted not going, and as I thought about it, I realized I was not too fond of the idea of playing football.

It differed from owning a business, working for myself, and writing or speaking. I have accomplished these things and more. I persisted through the doubt. It came up often, and I knew I could do everything.

I have owned four businesses, written nine books, produced movies, and helped others publish their books. I have created online training programs, consulted other business people, and presented my training programs. Along the way, doubt appeared. The difference was that I persisted through the dark times.

There were what I call now false starts. For example, in 1998, I wanted to return to my business and purchased a national sales training program license. After three years, deep down, I felt unfulfilled. Something was missing. I took on a partner to help me with the business, and I still felt the same. Two years later, life gave me a massive shove on November 13, 2002. One second I was doing a seminar, and the next, I needed an ambulance.

You've read earlier in this book that I'd had a sudden health crisis that day, and I can tell you that as I waited for the ambulance to arrive, I felt an immense wave of gratitude. I sensed that life gave me a flood or a forest fire to clear out everything. Though I was 100 days in the hospital and six months out of work, I was primarily grateful throughout the experience. The false start was that the national sales training license would never be my work. The feeling of being unfulfilled was my desire to do my work, and I was not going to achieve that as a franchise for someone else.

That began the new journey of starting what my work was. It was part-time while I worked with a former sales training client, and my business was full-time by 2013.

I have a story about a client I call "W" for this book.

W has persisted through the doubt in his mind and still does to this day. He noticed this in plain sight: every time life wasn't going according to "his plan," his default pattern was to think, "This isn't working, and I am going to fail." Doubt was his default pattern. People around him would notice his language become pessimistic—his view of what was possible was limited. With coaching, he looked back on his life and realized there were challenging times, and most of what he had feared did not come true. He had achieved more than he had imagined and had made more money. He learned that the results he desired appeared by persisting through the doubt.

Once W recognized his default pattern, he could overcome it, and others helped him. His employees, friends, and partners started to push back when he resorted to his pessimistic tendencies. He was his own worst enemy. His acorn brain, as I call it, was that little voice saying, "Times are tough, you won't make it, or the business will fail;" none of that was true. He decided to run that voice and not let it run him. Rainer Marie Rilke calls that voice "the little hooligan" and asks, "Will you let the little hooligan run you, or will you run it?"

W realized over time that he was not that voice. Many people say, "I am my own worst enemy." What is true is that voice, the acorn brain, is not you. It's the "little hooligan's voice," and noticing it is the first step in overcoming it.

W has had many wins along the way by choosing to run his life based upon thinking about what he wants more of and not allowing the acorn brain to run him.

Below is a story of persistence and faith written is his journal.

I'll call him "JR."

On April 18, 2018 I began the aforementioned journal as a public record of my attempt(s) to qualify for Boston.

It was purchased on the date of the running of the 122nd Boston Marathon. One year later, I was running as a qualified runner for the 123rd Boston Marathon & then requalified for the 125th. Below is my summary of lessons learned.

Timeline & significant dates:
- 04/16/2018   JR watch marathon on TV & purchased journal
- 04/18/2018   First entry in journal
- 08/27/2018   Qualify for Boston at Green River Marathon
- Oct-2018   Had my 4th retina surgery with "face down for 7 days" required (again).
- 04/15/209   Ran MY 1st Boston
- 11/10/2019   Requalified for Boston 2021

Lessons learned:

- Belief is key
  - Declare it, believe it, achieve it
- Discipline
  - Need mental toughness & consistency.
  - Set up habits so it's not all willpower.
  - Prepare for, and sometimes give into, weakness.
- Focus
  - Consistent action, moving in the direction of your dreams.
  - Plan-do-review and change when necessary.
- Specialization
  - Eliminate things that distract you from your goal.
    - Kardio Kick was my eliminate.
- Coaches
  - Listen to everybody for ideas & advise.
  - Adopt what works for you & discard the rest.
  - Remember life is an experiment of one.

Lessons learned (con't):
- Mental aspects
  - HUGE area, especially for big-stretch goals.
  - New beliefs are sometimes necessary.
  - Listen to feedback (and for physical goals, listen to your body)
  - "Monkey mind" which is racing thoughts trying to convince you to quit.
    - Can't get rid of it, ever. Do try to quiet it.
    - Welcome it and be curious where it came from.
    - Answer it with the phrase, "Thank you. I'm wondering what you are trying to teach me right now, BUT I'M NOT QUITTING!!!"
    - Distinguish between listening to your body versus listening to monkey-mind.
  - Expect a yo-yo of emotions. Good day running, top of the world. Bad run or worse, bail on run, feel like crap (same for business, or trying to start a family or…)
  - Dedication – excuse cycles. Celebrate wins and relax the discipline for same (slightly) but don't let your period of dedication become the excuse to undo all.
  - Balance – don't be so strict that you no longer enjoy life.
  - Positive self-talk. Be kind to yourself.
  - Mantras. Use them to reframe. My calf cramp late in a Marathon became the mantra, "my fast twitch muscles are kicking in…"
- Upward spiral
  - Achieve a goal, feel good, set another.
  - Life is meant to expand continuously.
  - Not always a straight line up, but it will be an upward spiral if you let it. Sometimes resting & regrouping, but always upward.

Quotes:
- Fatigue makes cowards of us all.
- Fatigue is the constant companion of the endurance athlete.
- If you want to go fast, you have to go fast.
- If you want to go fast, go alone. If you want to go far, go with others.
- Enjoy solitude.
- Embrace the suck.

Finally, note my journal is focused on running, but the lessons are focused on life. They can be applied universally to any challenge.

Feel free to share &/or use as need.

Thank you JR…

Back to my thoughts: If Jim's journal notes are not the definition of persistence, I don't know what is. Run the marathon of life in a similar fashion, run through the ups and downs as Jim describes and see what happens. Perhaps you will find the gifts that life is urging you to see or find. Embrace it all is the message of this book.

I recommend these books to help: *Are You Ready to Succeed* by Dr. Srikumar Rao, *Wise Mind, Open Mind* by Dr Roland Alexander.

10.
Generosity of Time, Talent, Heart, and Spirit and the Impact of Its Opposite

Living in a Universe and embracing life as it is by seeing it as a gift means I do when life calls me to give.

I haven't always seen it that way. Although I was always generous when friends said, "Why are you giving to that person?" I would step back sometimes. Since that time on November 18, 2002, I've never questioned the call. Whether it's a knock on my car window, someone on the street, or at work, I always cheerfully answer with whatever is requested. It's what I am to do with my remaining time here. I am not storing anything up here because I took nothing that day with me to what is next. My life review showed the impact I had on so many others with what was a limited view of generosity. I live moment to moment since I had no clue I would die the day what's next arrived.

None of us know the exact day and time. We hang onto our money, possessions, talent, and time tightly. It's as if we deny ourselves the abundance the Creator provides. Today, knowing the good I do is somehow etched onto the fabric of time, I embrace each opportunity to return the gifts the Universe has given me.

How do you feel when you do good? I have asked hundreds, maybe thousands, that question, and the answer has mostly been, "I feel great or good." Why?

Is it tied to the experience I had with my life review? Only the good I did in my life flashed before me during my life review. It seems to me that the good we do is the concern of the Infinite, God, whatever you call the Creative Life Force. In my experience, what humans call sin is our small-minded, judgmental voice and not the concern of God. We are here to fall and make mistakes so that we learn and grow.

It seems to me that the Universe has a sense of humor too. After going to the ATM for cash, it's then that at a rest area during my travels, someone will knock on my car window and ask for gas, a sandwich, or money. They often have a story about a lost wallet, debit card, or hard luck to share. I stop them today and say, "Just tell me how I can help and skip the story; I am here to help." After, I thank the Universe and say, "Thank you for allowing me to serve."

You don't need to study the Law of Attraction or the Laws of the Universe if you can wake up and embrace life as a gift. Instead of a story of woe, look at what reaches you as serving a purpose. One that stays with you forever.

Since we have free will, it's your choice. Please continue to make life a burden and complain or experiment with what I suggest. I have found it a fantastic journey learning to do good, knowing it sure has an impact.

This approach to living has added immense joy to my life, a level of happiness that eluded me until November 18, 2002.

As I have become more generous, the return to me has been tenfold.

While lying in the hospital, $24,000 came to me in the mail. Five job offers came between November 13 and January 15. One came from a client, Mike P., who called the first week of January and asked, "Hey Stevie, what are you doing?" I replied, "Mike, I have been in the hospital since November 13, and I don't know when I will get out or be cleared to work."

I will never forget his reply, "Stevie, I have a job for you, and I'll wait to fill it until you know." I said, "Mike, I don't know if I will give up my business yet." He again said, "Steve, I will wait."

It was uncanny because in April, while driving back from my doctor, who had just cleared me to work, Mike called again, "Steve, are you ready to go to work?" I replied, "Mike, I just left the doctor's office, and I am ready to go and have decided to accept work, except I need time to sell the business."

Mike replied, "How much time?" I said, "By the end of the year, I can also give you the time the job requires."

He said, "I have a plane ticket for you to join us on Sunday in Atlanta for our national sales meeting, and you have the job."

Mike was a great boss, and he later referred me to his clients when I started my consulting and training business again a few years later.

11.
THE GIFT OF RESISTANCE AND DIFFICULTY

In chapter 1, I touched briefly on resistance being a gift. Life provides us with the training required to get to what we desire. The pain in the diagram above shows that pain and suffering are where we amplify it and make it worse.

I have a story that reflects this perfectly. A friend I met while covering the Northeast for a national company had big dreams. I'll call him "P." P dreamed of owning his own business, and when we met he was the Purchasing Director for one of my clients. He declared his goal to me, and what followed was life providing the training.

He got an offer for an excellent job that included the opportunity to own 50 percent of the company one day. It checked off many of his boxes: a significant pay increase and the responsibility for the company's day-to-day operations. Four years later the owner called him in to say he was cutting back and let P go. He was disappointed; he did learn to get any offers of ownership in writing for the future and observe how the owner conducted himself. He learned much about leadership and operating a business. He later reflected on this job as a gift.

Next up was a quick stop at another family-owned company, a one-year sidestep.

Next, he accepted a similar position with a smaller, family-owned company. Three years later, a similar fate. He was continuing his training despite not enrolling in it. Life was providing it.

Eight years passed, and he looked at other ownership opportunities, and nothing inspired him.

Next, he had two job offers; neither included ownership, and both were great opportunities. The one he accepted was the same company where he'd taken the one-year sidestep noted above.

Four more years and excellent training for what he desired continued, and the life "school" was still functioning.

During this time, an acquaintance approached him to help with the operations of a small light bulb company. He took on the role part-time. Next, a long-time aging friend took ill, and P helped him with billing and shipping details and kept this man's business running while he dealt with the health challenges.

P was giving of his time and talent. Soon he was offered a partnership, and his friend realized his declining health would be an issue for the business.

After twelve years of training that he would not have signed up for willingly, he recalls those years as the resistance he needed to persist through and learn from. Looking at the diagram on the chapter opener. You can see how P left his comfort zone of jobs, went through the pain, and began manifesting his dream.

More opportunities have continued for P as he follows his calling. He is a full-time entrepreneur with multiple businesses. Each job provided him with excellent training and experience, giving him the wisdom to run his firm today.

If you had told him you had a twelve-year course for business excellence, do you think he would have enrolled?

Life is always working for us. It's in plain sight. Most people stay stuck in "victim" thinking and describing how they suffer each day to anyone who listens. Embracing life as it is can be a choice that accepts all that shows up as meant for us. As Mohammed once said, "What has reached you was never meant to miss you, and what has missed you was never meant to reach you."

You have to prove this idea of resistance being a gift from life as a necessary part of getting you to your goal—gratitude and awe for the blessing of living in a miracle is one step.

I learned this from nearly dying. Before that day in November 2002, I was silently bitter that life wasn't working out "my way." I was asleep to how life was preparing me for what I desired. Since that day, I have been grateful for all my life, especially the challenges. I can see what I previously missed. As the Apostle Paul once said, "And we know that for those who love God all things work together for good, for those who are called according to his purpose" (Rom. 8.28, ESV). I see that and am grateful for everything and "in" everything that happens.

You can use that when you don't feel particularly grateful for something, be thankful "in" it. It is life training you, preparing you for the desires you have and the goals you have set.

When coaching anyone today, I listen for the declaration of what they want. I urge my clients to think of "limitless possibilities" and then pay attention to "what wants to happen." When I ask, "Could this be life training you?" Get this concept and get excited that you are heading toward your goals.

I will leave you with this quote from Ernest Holmes, "I have an Infinite Companion who goes with me wherever I go. I have a partnership with the Infinite that is steady and strong and certain" (*Science of Mind*).

12.
THE PATH GIVEN

Deepak Chopra says, "Even when you think you have your life all mapped out, things happen that shape your destiny in ways you might have never imagined."

Two days in 2002, November 13–14 , shaped me in ways I'd never imagined and brought my calling with them. I suggest that life provides us with our true calling and that most of us miss it. How many people do you know who stay safe and never risk taking steps toward their true desires? How many people complain about their lives, mates, jobs, or "shit" that happened to them? The "shit" that happened to them was their calling. Life attempted to shape a new destiny for them, and because it didn't fit "their map," they missed it. It's been said that the wealthiest places on earth are the cemeteries, where so many unrealized dreams are buried.

Today my life is about my calling, which continues to open in ways beyond anything I have imagined.

I was the licensee for a national sales training program. I was ecstatic when I purchased the license four years earlier, in 1998. I was sure this was my calling and, initially, I embraced it. Life had another idea. A part of me died that day on November 18 and I was reborn into my calling. I knew after three years that the national sales program I was conducting was missing something. I added the idea that we live in a miracle

Universe. I was urging my clients to experiment with changing themselves. My quote, "If you don't like your experience of the world, change how the world is experiencing you," came from that work. "Prove this to yourselves, don't take my word for it," I said often. "All the techniques and tactics in the world won't help you in sales if you are inauthentic," I barked as clients worked through role play. I wasn't sure how to extricate myself from this license, and life took care of that.

On November 13, one second I was standing in front of my clients, helping them prepare for the day's class, and the next, I needed an ambulance. Sixty days straight (except for Thanksgiving evening) in the hospital and forty days out of the following sixty were the beginning. Six months out of work, friends urged me to give up the license. Initially, I resisted the idea, although it felt like I had to restart the business after this ordeal. I sold the client list to other licensees, negotiated commissions on any referral from my clients, and started my work part-time after I accepted a job from another of my clients. I conducted my work every Monday evening, and many of my original clients signed up for the class, and *Voila*, Lord & Lentini was born, and I haven't looked back. Life provided me with the path, and I surrendered to it. I would have missed what was in plain sight if I had continued to insist on keeping the license.

Thank you, Universe, and thank you, Infinite Wisdom. I am grateful every day for this gift and for what has unfolded. I meet the most amazing people and travel all over the country, sharing my message.

Where are you missing that is in plain sight? The more challenging it seems, the greater the gift.

Here is a story about a guy I'll call "R."

At age fifteen, his father passed away from cancer. R resolved at this time to study oncology and become an oncologist. That seemed not to work, and he took a few jobs in the medical device world. Eventually, he landed at a company whose main work was infusion devices for chemotherapy. Today he is the CEO of that company living out his passion for helping others overcome cancer. While not becoming an oncologist might have seemed like a disappointment, it was actually the case that life had a different idea about how he could serve.

The following example is "WG."

WG grew up around the ocean. Curious as a lad, always asking questions of many things and especially fisherman. At age four, his dad taught him how to row a boat. WG loved the water. Fast-forward, he studied fisheries management. His roommate got a 4' 55-gallon fish tank, so WG went out and got a fish tank. Soon the third roommate got many smaller tanks and started breeding fish. In plain sight his life, his life's work was unfolding. WG says, "Happiest people are sexy because they love their life."

His first job was with government at the Fisheries Management Bureau. Boring. He was obsessing about reef tanks, and his dad said one day, "Be bold, call the New England Aquarium and ask to speak with the Director." It was a Saturday, and the Director picked up the phone because it was a Saturday. WG explained what he'd studied, where he worked, and that he loved reef tanks and dreamed of working at the Aquarium. They met a few days later, and two weeks after that, WG had a temporary job there; three months later, it was a permanent one.

Three-and-a-half years later, a homeowner needed help with a saltwater tank, leading to a few more clients. Eventually, that led to consulting for the Lisbon Aquarium in Portugal and, little by little, it was the start of his aquarium business. That work led to his work at the Ocean Explorium, which was his "path given." Many of the people he met early on in his career were instrumental along his path. The Ocean Explorium work came from the same guy who took him to Portugal, and all that came from a chance meeting at a conference. If you think your life is out of order, reflect on where life has taken you. Each event and or person is a guide to what our calling is. It can even change three or more times in life, and the experience of each is preparation for what is to come.

WG arrived at his latest gift, mentoring young people through the experience at the Ocean Explorium as he mentored his employees and the many young people that interned there. He also came to this with the death of his son at age fifteen. WG came to wake him one morning, and he had passed. There was no reason except he died in his sleep. In addition to his mentoring podcast, WG is successfully raising funds to help young people reach their dreams as performing artists in memory of his son. His son was an exceptional talent, a genius in many ways, and life has given WG the task of helping many others, which is his calling. I am blessed and grateful to know WG and his wife and to have met his son.

Often, life's gifts do not come wrapped as we would like. Some come in our darkest moments, and take a while to see them. When storms and challenges come, it's hard to know the gift initially, and some never find it as they rail against what occurred.

In my experience, with the shift in consciousness to searching for the gift, you will find more joy than spending time telling the story of how miserable events have just ruined your life.

13.
WAKING UP TO LIFE AS FEEDBACK

Life is feedback. That is a bold statement for most of us. In today's society, most people prefer to rail against what occurs in their lives that doesn't fit their picture, which I call the victim mode. It is small-minded limited thinking stuck in a rut.

Life is feedback for "masters of circumstances." They wake up to what each circumstance's gift is. It might be to learn and grow. The mirror might show them something they have not seen in themselves.

Embracing life as it is, requires the belief that the Universal Creator, whatever you call it, presents you with a gift in every moment. Rainer Maria Rilke once said, "And as for the rest, let life happen to you. Believe me: life is in the right." Jesus said, "Everything works together for good" (Rom. 8.28). Mohammed said, "What has reached you was never meant to miss you, and what has missed you was never meant to reach you."

It's a different mindset that looks at everything that occurs and every person in our lives as a gift.

The Universe is arranged perfectly in this galaxy; everything required for life to occur on earth is here.

Is that not the case in our lives? How could that be?

Our hubris and egoic mind, the acorn brain as I call it, has us thinking the reverse. That everything in our life or much of it is out of order.

Life as feedback and a gift is something that you have to prove to yourself. Make your life an experiment by thinking, *Ok, this has reached me; that means it's meant for me.* As Mohammed said, "let me find the gift or the lesson."

More ways to help you with this concept are in Eckhart Tolle's Ten Principles in the following chapter.

I have a story to share about feedback being a gift.

A man I will call "D" was described by many as a "bull in a China shop." He had no idea how his behavior was impacting those around him. He was oblivious to the impact he had on others. He wasn't listening, pushing back everywhere, and his perception was he was right. People around him were reluctant to give him any feedback. What occurred was what I call the "perception gap." Life can provide feedback from those who are willing to risk our wrath. If all of life is in perfect order, then our job is to speak up and take that risk if we can help others see what is in plain sight.

As I coached various people who worked with or for D, I would hear people complain about some of his behaviors and suggest that they share their feedback with him directly. Six months passed, and I listened to the same complaints always asking, "Did you share that feedback with D?"

The answer was no. When we complain to others about others, we help no one. It's gossip. When we complain directly, I call it a "complaint with a request to the person or people who can do something about it." As the complaints continued, I told everyone complaining about D, "If you don't tell him, I will." That is what I did. After I shared with D what he needed to hear, his first reaction was to feel confronted and hurt. My first reaction to feedback was similar.

Today, people share with me that D has changed, that he is open, receptive, a good listener, and a good leader. Life, through others, provided feedback that D needed to hear. He heard it and changed. When feedback comes from love, it's a gift. Love is helping others listen to what they need to hear and risking they will no longer embrace you. Our best friends in life will risk our wrath. Those we love sometimes will not share the truth, which, in my family's case, is not helpful on our journey. I urge people to share what seems problematic, as it may be the best gift. I suggest it is the best gift you can give anyone.

Where are you holding back honest feedback that could be helpful?

Where are you looking at loving someone as being gentle with them?

How could honest feedback help someone immensely, and yet you hold back?

Be kind, clear, and loving by sharing what might risk their wrath.

D would agree; life is feedback.

14.
Eckhart Tolle's Ten Principles

Eckhart Tolle says in his book, *A New Earth,*

Life will give you whatever experience is most helpful for the evolution of your consciousness. How do you know this is the experience you need? Because this is the experience you are having at the moment.. . . Response-ability—the ability to respond.

"He says,

> To awaken, it is important to know that there is no such thing as an ordinary moment. There are only two kinds of moments: Life is either inviting you to be fully open to life right here and right now, or it is putting you in the situations that are needed to bring up what has been bound up inside of you so you can open it up, and be free. **The Ship** —by Steve Lentini
>
> Savor . . . slower . . . life is fast
>
> Like a ship crashing against turbulent waves
>
> Emotional storms, thundering flashes of brilliance, and raging wildfires, no shore in sight
>
> Navigating barely tightly gripping what?

A steering wheel is the illusion.

Captain absent

Diving in optional

The storm is in charge

Darkest hour before the dawning

Hanging on hope abounds Land Ho!

Eckhart also says, "When you fight life, life fights you."

Eckhart Tolle's 10 Rules for Success Are:

1. Take the small steps that lead to greatness.
2. Enjoy the journey.
3. Find satisfaction in your work.
4. Ask the right questions.
5. Find your inner purpose.
6. Direct your attention.
7. Be compassionate with yourself; don't get stuck in unhappiness.
8. Don't get stuck in unhappiness.
9. Contribute to a better world.
10. Change your state of consciousness.

Watch this video on the 10 Rules for Success on YouTube:

https://www.youtube.com/watch?v=w6JdJeu9ziw

Tolle describes the 10 Rules far better than I could—click the link and enjoy this moment.

15.
LIVING WITH AN OPEN MIND

This chapter is all quotes, many of my favorites. The passages of many others make my argument for living with an open mind much better than anything I would write. Consider this advice from these people, whom I call Sages, and notice how their quotes call us to embrace life as it is. I urge you to consider life a gift, not a burden, as something to live in awe and amazement instead of something to "fight and overcome." It's your choice.

Consider the book by Roland Alexander, Ph.D., *Wise Mind Open Mind*, and below is a link to the book on Goodreads.
https://www.goodreads.com/book/show/6549922-wise-mind-open-mind?ac=1&from_search=true&qid=xV4WStOJky&rank=5

> All sons of Adam are part of one single body.
>
> They are of the same essence.
>
> When time afflicts us with pain
>
> In one part of that body
>
> All the other parts feel it too.
>
> If you fail to feel the pain of others

You do not deserve the name of man. —Saadi Shirazi is the author of those luminous verses that now stand at the entrance of the headquarters of the United Nations.

"Never follow anyone or anything blindly."
"Common sense has given way to 'experts.'"

—Steve Lentini

"We must be willing to let go of the life we planned so as to have the life that is waiting for us."

—Joseph Campbell

Your assumptions are your windows on the world. Scrub them off every once in a while, or the light won't come in."

—Alan Alda

"Those who cannot change their minds cannot change anything."

—George Bernard Shaw

Who is more humble? The scientist who looks at the universe with an open mind and accepts whatever the universe has to teach us, or somebody who says everything in this book must be considered the literal truth and never mind the fallibility of all the human beings involved?

—Carl Sagan

"A mind is like a parachute. It doesn't work if it is not open."

—Frank Zappa

Life moves on, whether we act as cowards or heroes. Life has no other discipline to impose, if we would but realize it, than to accept life unquestioningly. Everything we shut our eyes to, everything we run away from, everything we deny, denigrate or despise, serves to defeat us in the end. What seems nasty, painful, evil, can become a source of beauty, joy, and strength, if faced with an open mind. Every moment is a golden one for him who has the vision to recognize it as such."

—Henry Miller

"I will not be 'famous,' 'great.' I will go on adventuring, changing, opening my mind and my eyes, refusing to be stamped and stereotyped. The thing is to free one's self: to let it find its dimensions, not be impeded."

—Virginia Woolf

"Minds are like flowers, they only open when the time is right."

—Stephen Richard

"The art of living . . . is neither careless drifting on the one hand nor fearful clinging to the past on the other. It consists in being sensitive to each moment, in regarding it as utterly new and unique, in having the mind open and wholly receptive."

—Alan Wilson Watts

Very few beings really seek knowledge in this world. Mortal or immortal, few really ask. On the contrary, they try to wring from the unknown the answers they have already shaped in their own minds—justifications, confirmations, forms of consolation without which they can't go on. To really ask is to open the door to the whirlwind. The answer may annihilate the question and the questioner.

—Anne Rice

"There are just lots of possibilities in the world . . . I need to keep my mind open for what could happen and not decide that the world is hopeless if what I want to happen doesn't happen. Because something else great might happen in between."

—Rachel Cohn

From time to time, sit close to the one you love, hold his or her hand, and ask, "Darling, do I understand you enough, or am I making you suffer? Please tell me so that I can learn to love you properly. I don't want to make you suffer, and if I do so because of my ignorance, please tell me so that I can love you better, so that you can be happy." If you say this in a voice that communicates your real openness to understand, the other person may cry.

That is a good sign, because it means the door of understanding is opening and everything will be possible again.

—Thich Nhat Hanh

"If your mind is empty, it is always ready for anything, it is open to everything. In the beginner's mind there are many possibilities, but in the expert's mind there are few."

—Shunryu Suzuki

When you open yourself to the continually changing, impermanent, dynamic nature of your own being and of reality, you increase your capacity to love and care about other people and your capacity to not be afraid. You're able to keep your eyes open, your heart open, and your mind open. And you notice when you get caught up in prejudice, bias, and aggression. You develop an enthusiasm for no longer watering those negative seeds, from now until the day you die. And, you begin to think of your life as offering endless opportunities to start to do things differently.

—Pema Chödrön

"Keep your mind open. The meaning of things lies in how people perceive them. The same thing could mean different meanings to the same people at different times."

—Roy T. Bennett

It does take great maturity to understand that the opinion we are arguing for is merely the hypothesis we favor, necessarily imperfect, probably transitory, which only very limited minds can declare to be a certainty or a truth.

—Milan Kundera

"Keep an open mind; it's the only way new things can get in."

—Colleen Hoover

Throughout human history, as our species has faced the frightening, terrorizing fact that we do not know who we are, or where we are going in this ocean of chaos, it has been the authorities, the political, the religious, the educational authorities who attempted to comfort us by giving us order, rules, regulations, informing, forming in our minds their view of reality. To think for yourself you must question authority and learn how to put yourself in a state of vulnerable, open-mindedness; chaotic, confused, vulnerability to inform yourself.

—Timothy Leary

16.
WE SHOULDN'T CALL DEATH, DEATH

I could hear an indescribable seething roar which wasn't in my ear but everywhere and had nothing to do with sounds. I realized that I had died and been reborn numberless times but just didn't remember especially because the transitions from life to death and back to life are so ghostly easy, a magical action for naught, like falling asleep and waking up again a million times, the utter casualness and deep ignorance of it. I realized it was only because of the stability of the intrinsic Mind that these ripples of birth and death took place, like the action of the wind on a sheet of pure, serene, mirror-like water. I felt sweet, swinging bliss, like a big shot of heroin in the mainline vein; like a gulp of wine late in the afternoon and it makes you shudder; my feet tingled. I thought I was going to die the very next moment. But I didn't die.

—Jack Kerouac

On November 13, 2002, I proceeded to my everyday work: teaching salespeople who were my clients. One minute I was fine; the next, I needed an ambulance. Immediately I was admitted to the ICU, and five days later I flatlined.

The last thing I remember about this earthly life was my two friends at the end of my hospital bed. Then, I became "one with everything and nothing," although my consciousness remained. I was one with the Infinite, the Life Force. Lao Tzu said in the *Dao De Ching* (some call it the *Tao Te Ching*) it had no name, no religion, no sex, no race, nothing from what I now call my acorn brain—nothing from here was there. Lao explained, "The Tao that can be told is not the eternal Tao. The name that can be named is not the eternal Name. The unnamable is the eternally real. Naming is the origin of all particular things."

Next, I experienced a full life review and every day since I recall it in amazement. Only the good I had done and the moments when I had positively touched someone's life flashed before me. All the family, friends, and strangers I had helped and all the good I had done were part of this fabric of time.

Think about that, how do you feel when you do good? How do you feel when you help someone or cheer someone?

And then, a decision.

Next, a voice I cannot describe to this day asked, "Stay or go?" At that moment, my soul surrendered with "Thy will be done."

October, I was a fifty-year-old man who had never fully surrendered that way. I lived mainly in the past and the future, reviewing mistakes or wanting something other than what the moment brought; on November 18 all that changed.

Immediately after my soul surrendered to what Lao Tzu calls "the Tao," I awakened to find myself back in the ICU. I wasn't sure what day it was, just that I was in and out of consciousness. Later, I asked the two friends visiting me, "What had they seen? Had I appeared strange or different?" They answered, "Oh, that was Monday the 18th at 2ish, The doctors and nurses came rushing in as the vital alarms went off," They said, "Out, out, this is it, call his family."

That was just the first five days—which turned into 100 days in the hospital over the next five months, sixty days straight—one day home on Thanksgiving and back in the hospital the next day—forty days out of the next ninety days! I was grateful for it all. I even had a sense of gratitude wash over me in the ambulance. I felt that this event was like a flood or a forest fire and that afterwards a new growth would come.

Like many others, I survived two health challenges that could have killed me! The first is called Acute Necrotizing Pancreatitis. The second is an Anterior Myocardial Infarction. I invite you to look them up to understand their significance and life-threatening danger.

And please remember, all this occurred in a flash without warning. I had never had any symptoms: just boom, hospitalization. But what a gift it was.

> **We shouldn't call death, death; we should call it "what's next."**
>
> —by Steve Lentini

Death came and knocked on my door without realizing it, I had left the door open.

Death came in uninvited and stayed awhile.

There I was, stuck, in the past or the future, not yet formed, and death invited me to take a walk and showed me what my life had meant to many.

While on the way to where I do not know, death asked me, "Stay or go"?

I answered with a total surrender to the moment with, "Thy will be done."

And back in intensive care; only then could I put together all the moments that had just occurred.

Death was one with everything and nothing and was a lie. There was no death, only what was next and next and next. I am here now in this next and unafraid of what is next.

I missed that there is only what is next after death.

Essential Everyday Reminders to Smooth Our Way

My experience of "what's next" clarified several essential differences between this world and the next. Below are the most helpful, actionable lessons I took away. Each day, I try to remember and live by them, except when my acorn brain attempts to hijack my thinking! Perhaps one or all will resonate with you and provide help as you journey along your path.

1. We live in a miracle, a mystery, and are always one with the infinite.
2. Nothing from here is where we head next. Like a drop of water in the ocean, you become a part of everything and nothing. Titles, material possessions, sins—none of what I thought mattered so much here—only the good we do.
3. Divisions such as sex, race, nationalities, sexual preferences exist only here. We must learn and grow in this place by over-coming our small-minded thinking. Our job here is to do good and become more like the infinite thinker in us all.
4. Only the moment, the present, is guaranteed. The Divine or the infinite or God (no matter what you call it) resides in the now. I was here, then there, and back in a single moment. I could not string the events together until I was back in my body in the ICU. This unique experience taught me that the Divine, God,

is always with us. I learned that everyone and everything is here to teach me something. I don't have to search for God, God is in the moment, and I accept all that enters my life as good and for a reason.

The Key Is to Live from the InsideOut™.

Death is a myth. As many of the sages have suggested, we are eternal. Most small-minded, egoic brains don't get that part very well. Rather than hearing our inner voice, we live mainly from the "outside-in," seeking validation or material things to satisfy us. Essentially, we rely on what we see and hear to guide our thoughts and actions and give our lives meaning.

What if we lived from the "InsideOut ™" instead? What would that look like, and how could it be beneficial? Living from the inside out instead of from the outside means thinking, "Today, I'll be happy and satisfied." If you decide that, then outside influences won't move you. As a fellow human being, I can say this is the most challenging part: not reacting.

Seek your proof and truth.

Some say we always see what we believe. That idea suggests that each of us has the power to create, manifest, and take responsibility for what life brings. Prove that concept to yourself. Ask, "Do I believe that what I see is all there is to know? Or is this person, event, or experience here to teach me something?"

Start your day by committing to viewing your life as the observer. Decide that nothing and no one external will take away your joy because you are the creator of your experience. When you find this difficult to do—or perhaps impossible—remember that, as many sages have said, "This too shall pass," and ask "What in this could I be grateful for?"

Surrender to the Present Moment

Although it's hard to remember, and our acorn brain often gets in the way, my experience showed me that we must focus on making the most of each moment. The now really is all we have. We must embrace and accept it. Many of us told our children, when they left for school each morning, "Make good choices." That is excellent advice for us all.

Consider how clearly and eloquently Tolle makes the same argument—and shows the importance of rejecting the "my mind made me" stories we so often tell ourselves: https://www.oprah.com/oprahs-lifeclass/eckhart-tolles-10-powerful- insights-to-a-happier-you

Tolle says two things that remind us to surrender, "Some people think the reality is nuts." And, "If you fight life, life fights you" (Eckhart Tolle, *The Power of Now*).

The beauty of what's next is that only the now, the present moment, exists there. "What's next" contains only the Divine, God, the infinite (it doesn't matter what you call it), and nothing else. I learned that all life is the creative life force flowing through us and that this force exists in all the moments we love and all those we resist. In the moments we fight, we miss the lesson. As Ben Franklin said, "A person wrapped up in themselves makes a very small bundle."

It's Time to Do the Hard Work

Will you question your answers in life? Will you give up victim thinking? Can you take responsibility for what shows up in your life? Will you open up to the folly of following anyone or anything mindlessly?

Think about what Einstein said about the creative force, the superior reasoning power that created this incomprehensible Universe. Will you leave behind small-minded, limited thinking and the idea of wanting everyone to be the same or think the same, rejecting all those who disagree with your point of view?

Take a chance. See what happens when you fully experiment with being in the moment, going with the flow no matter what. Like me, I believe you will prove that you can experience life in fantastic ways when you change. Please, don't just take my word for it! As you read this book, I think you will find much of the sage advice will mirror what I am saying.

Read about what Baruch Spinoza says about God below. He wrote this in the 1600s, so I had to suspend editing and grammar check. Grammarly had forty-one issues with his writing, and I decided to present it to you as he wrote it. Suspend your corn brain" and take in what he suggests.

Spinoza writes,

> God would say:
>
> Stop praying.
>
> What I want you to do is go out into the world and enjoy your life. I want you to sing, have fun and enjoy everything I've made for you.
>
> Stop going into those dark, cold temples that you built yourself and saying they are my house. My house is in the mountains, in the woods, rivers, lakes, beaches. That's where I live, and there I express my love for you.
>
> Stop blaming me for your miserable life; I never told you there was anything wrong with you or that you were a sinner, or that your sexuality was a bad thing. Sex is a gift I have given you and with which you can express your love, your ecstasy, your joy. So don't blame me for everything they made you believe.
>
> Stop reading alleged sacred scriptures that have nothing to do with me. If you can't read me in a sunrise, in a landscape, in

the look of your friends, in your son's eyes … you will find me in no book!

Stop asking me "will you tell me how to do my job?" Stop being so scared of me. I do not judge you or criticize you, nor get angry, or bothered. I am pure love.

Stop asking for forgiveness, there's nothing to forgive. If I made you… I filled you with passions, limitations, pleasures, feelings, needs, inconsistencies… free will. How can I blame you if you respond to something I put in you? How can I punish you for being the way you are, if I'm the one who made you? Do you think I could create a place to burn all my children who behave badly for the rest of eternity? What kind of God would do that?

Respect your peers and don't do what you don't want for yourself. All I ask is that you pay attention in your life, that alertness is your guide.

My beloved, this life is not a test, not a step on the way, not a rehearsal, nor a prelude to paradise. This life is the only thing here and now and it is all you need.

I have set you absolutely free, no prizes or punishments, no sins or virtues, no one carries a marker, no one keeps a record.

You are absolutely free to create in your life. Heaven or hell.

I can't tell you if there's anything after this life but I can give you a tip. Live as if there is not. This is your only chance to enjoy, love, and exist.

So, if there's nothing after, then you will have enjoyed the opportunity I gave you. And if there is, rest assured that I won't ask if you behaved right or wrong, I'll ask. Did you like it? Did you have fun? What did you enjoy the most? What did you learn?…

Stop believing in me; believing is assuming, guessing, imagining. I don't want you to believe in me. I want you to believe in you. I want you to feel me in you when you kiss your beloved, when you tuck in your little girl, when you caress your dog, when you bathe in the sea.

Stop praising me. What kind of egomaniac God do you think I am?

I'm bored being praised. I'm tired of being thanked. Feeling grateful? Prove it by taking care of yourself, your health, your relationships, the world. Express your joy! That's the way to praise me.

Stop complicating things and repeating as a parakeet what you've been taught about me.

What do you need more miracles for? So many explanations?

The only thing for sure is that you are here, that you are alive, that this world is full of wonders" (Baruch Spinoza, *God of Spinoza*).

"And by the way, stop worrying about sin and living in fear." God of Spinoza

The other major lesson I learned was that sin is a myth—a human construction from the small-minded thinker. In this Universe, we pay here for any negative actions. Life itself is feedback. Some pay with jail time or financial consequences. Others with embarrassment, regret, and guilt. Also, it's small-minded to want "them" to "burn in hell forever."

God does not think like us; that idea is our hubris. Learning, growing, and feeling more like the Divine is our job.

Living to avoid death is not living. Expecting others to protect us from death is folly. We all leave here for what's next, and as many sages have said, "What reaches us is meant for us, and what misses us wasn't."*

*Mohammed 570–632 AD said, " What has reached you was never meant to miss you, and what has missed you was never meant to reach you."

Just as I didn't know what was coming on November 13, 2002 (the ambulance and ICU), you'll have no clue when your time comes, and it reached me. Whether it's a diagnosis, an accident, or a sudden death, all are great reasons to enjoy the moment. Live your life anger free, and accept what comes. I wish my readers a long life, of course, and some of you may experience "what's next" before finishing this book or on the way to the bookstore.

Choose action, not reaction.

I encourage you to take advantage of the lessons I've learned and shared here. Consider changing your life to live daily by following the advice the sages have provided for thousands of years. Read my book *Sage Advice – Wisdom for Living from Throughout the Ages*. Buy it by clicking on this Amazon link; https://www.amazon.com/author/stevelentini.

Or any of my other books here as well. https://www.amazon.com/author/stephenlentini

Did these wise people have a "knowing" or perhaps a glimpse of what's next like I did? I'm not sure. My passage there and back gave me the fantastic gift of seeing and being with what gave us life. So, I urge you: to enjoy this miracle, take care of the earth, and work to leave everyone and everything a little better than you find them.

Do Good.

If we knew what awaited us, we would leave behind all of our pettiness and greed. Instead of small-minded thinking, judgment, and anger, we would focus on doing good and working to leave everyone and everything a little better than we find them in this temporary existence. Just think, we are space travelers on a rock for a ship, hurtling through an infinite void called a Universe. This is a miracle in itself, and that thought alone could be the reminder that anything small-minded does not come from whatever created this miracle.

Consider the following wisdom that, for me, validates the experience I had on November 18, 2002. https://www.sci-nature.vip/2021/09/quantum-theory-proves-that.html#

17.
THE CLUES THAT NATURE PROVIDES

Seeds contain everything within them to grow under the right conditions. They know what to do when planted at the correct depth, watered, fed, cared for, and nothing else is required. We, too, have inside us all that is needed; it's just not as automatic as a seed. Discovering what is ours to do in this life is more complicated. We tend to rail against what occurs in our life and complain instead of embracing what shows up as life nudging us to the path. Life is feedback once you accept it as divine or from the creative life force.

In the late 1980s, near the small town of Oracle, Arizona, just north of Tucson, scientists built Biosphere 2 (Biosphere 1 is the earth) at the cost of $200 million. Early in the 1990s, eight people committed to living there for two years. It was a failure, but the scientists did learn a lot.

The trees were growing horizontally instead of vertically. Sunlight was plentiful since the Biosphere was all glass, and the trees were weak, creeping, and low to the ground. Trees need to withstand wind to grow healthy and strong; the stronger the wind, the stronger the tree.

Many humans do the reverse. We use any means of escape to avoid storms: alcohol, drugs, sex, video gaming, and binge-watching TV, to name a few, when difficulty arises. We miss the opportunity to grow healthier and stronger in the storms.

I complained to anyone listening about the "storms" that arose: relationships, bosses, businesses, and any part of my life that didn't match the "perfect picture" I had. I missed the opportunity to grow and forgot what was in plain sight. I was a victim of circumstances, not the master of my circumstances.

Today, society and government want us to live without challenges and fix many past mistakes. A utopian vision of how life should be "storm- or challenge-free." In 2000, I embarked on a path of more profound growth. I hired a coach and looked at how I created all the events in my life and the gift they were giving. At forty-eight, I embraced life and was grateful for the new attitude. I was grateful as I waited for the ambulance on November 13, 2002. I knew life presented a significant gift, although I didn't know how large.

Everything you think, do, and say is a seed to a future harvest. How are you preparing the ground for your future harvest? Are you locked in "victim" or "why me" thinking? Imagine the harvest that thinking like that will bring about.

What are your predominant thoughts and words? These are the seeds of your future harvest.

What does your harvest look like based on your recent thoughts and words?

Are you even thinking about your future harvest?

Begin thinking now:

What crops have you planted through the years?

What crops have you planted in the past year?

What crops would you plant now?

What farmer would prepare a crop without considering what they wanted to harvest first? Would corn appear without planting corn seeds? Isn't it interesting that we humans wish for new things in our lives, yet we are planting the same old seeds all the time and expecting a new harvest just the same? How will you get a new harvest if you do not change your thoughts, words, and actions?

It's impossible, in fact, ridiculous, to expect a tomato when you planted squash. A new harvest only comes when we sow with new thoughts, words, and actions.

Prepare the ground. Think positive thoughts; surround yourself with others that support your vision. Spend quiet time meditating and visualizing your new future, your new harvest. Start with the end in mind. See the harvest you desire and work backward to make a general outline for its manifestation. Sign up for training courses designed to help you grow as an individual. Make sure, too, that you also plan time for some rest. These steps prepare the ground for your new future, just like farmers have a plan to prepare the soil.

Plant the seeds. Your thoughts, words, and actions must align with your planned harvest. Act as if you already have what you want. Once you plant the seeds, relax until the sprouts appear. Trust, have faith that things are working "underground" until those first signs of the shoots emerge.

Take time to visualize those seeds pushing through the ground of past habits and resistance.

Tend to the sprouts. This is the tender stage of your harvest. Ensure your shoots do not get trampled on, eaten, or frozen. The next step is where you persist through the high winds, rain, and spring mud. Things may look messy at the early stage of planting a new idea or harvest, and we stay with it no matter what!

Hold the vision and keep focused on the intention. What is your vision? What is your intention?

Weed, feed, and water. Watch for pests. Now you are at the stage where you fight off doubt. You keep an eye on what you planted. It's not the time for rest; stay in the fields hard at work. Pay attention; be disciplined with your thinking, words, and action. Disciplined and focused people get what they want. Be patient as well. Would you stand over a tomato plant after it was sprouted and shout, "Hey, give me a tomato now?" No, you would not. Everything has its cycle, be patient. Your ideas have a natural cycle as well.

As you would tend a garden, you must tend to your body, mind, and spirit.

How are you doing that?

Name the ways. Name at least three ways for the three aspects: body, mind, and spirit.

If you trouble with this, then ask others how they do it or talk to your coach or group or partner. Write down their replies. Ask at least three people.

Gather the harvest and take notes on what you reaped. Did it fit your plan? If not, reflect on what happened. Be prepared to let go of things that did not work. Like the trees let go of their leaves in fall, this is your time to let things go. Elimination is what nature does during autumn and many other times; maybe that's why dinosaurs are not still here.

Note what did work and plan to repeat it. Nature does the same here as well.

Nature doesn't waste anything; we do. We miss the gift by not modeling the gift of seeds, the patience for the process, and the seasons.

We go through hardships and difficulties just as any creature or crop does. The difference is that we have the acorn brain, the small-minded thinking working to scare us. Governments and religious leaders use fear to master us, knowing that it activates our "acorn brain." In my near-death experience, as stated earlier in this book, there was no heaven or hell, only the next moment, one with the infinite, one with everything and nothing. One with the limitless and none of my limited, small-minded thinking went with me.

Do you think the force that created this fantastic Universe is a small-minded thinker? That the Creator of trillions of life forms has one favorite religion or one preferred sex, or one preferred sexual preference. When we make anything wrong here, we are making the Creator unsuitable. What is in plain sight is for us to learn to embrace and accept our journey and leave all others for their journeys. The journey of others is none of my business anymore; my journey is not any of your business.

We see leaders at every level of government pointing the finger of blame instead of accepting responsibility and being accountable for what occurs. They model this poor behavior and expect the general population to behave differently. We must elect new leaders who model behaviors that encourage dialogue with the goal of compromise. Leaders who accept and embrace the differences that all of us have. We need to elect leaders who embrace doing the right thing instead of being right. We need at least two more US political parties and term limits. The concept of career politician has failed us. Other parties would mean that each Congress would have to negotiate with others and have a dialogue to reach a majority to rule. Term limits would mean more citizens would have to step up and serve.

Let's fund elections at the Federal Level and eliminate the "large donor" concept and fundraising currently required of politicians. Give each candidate at the federal level the same funding. Eliminate lobbying and make selling influence by friends and relatives of members of Congress a crime.

Imagine how the media would resist the idea of limiting funding for elections. Think of the billions of dollars that all the outlets receive through political ads. Perhaps that would eliminate the reporting "to fit a narrative" and encourage a return to real journalism based on fact.

I know that what I am suggesting is a complete overhaul of our system, and until then, I accept in a democracy what the outcome is of every election and do what I can to change things. I no longer spend time railing against what is because nature doesn't. Nature moves along no matter what. Once I learned to do the same thing, my life became filled with joy, at least more. I still have the acorn brain trying daily to run me, and primarily, I run it.

Please don't take my word for it; prove to yourself that life is a gift, stretching us beyond our small-minded limited thinking into limitless, infinite thinking like the force that created this miracle.

Did the Universal Creator make us different for us to learn and grow? Is it our job to learn to embrace each other?

Begin with the end in mind and work backward. Being awake to the gift that life is starts with you. Your life is the total of your thoughts, words, and actions up to this point. Do you desire a different outcome? Do you see yourself able to achieve great things and yet it hasn't happened, or have you seen many difficulties along the way? Somewhere your actions and your thinking have created this. Take full responsibility for it and begin anew—model people who have achieved what you want. Ask them to mentor you. Hang around those people.

Visualize your new future and work backward. Plant the seeds of that future you desire. Be bold and venture out, honoring that desire. That desire is the seed that the Universe gifted you with; until you celebrate that, you will feel unfulfilled. That feeling is the Universe nudging you to get started. Plant that seed and follow the steps that nature has in plain sight.

Persist through the doubt, the storms, and the challenges, and watch what happens with your life. Embrace all that comes because it is a necessary part of the path.

18.
CHANGE YOUR STATE OF CONSCIOUSNESS—THE LAW OF GROWTH

"You do not become good by trying to be good, but by finding the goodness that is already within you, and allowing that goodness to emerge. But it can only emerge if something fundamental changes in your state of consciousness."

— Eckhart Tolle.

Something Ernest Holmes said applies to me:

You cannot in one bound, in one jump, expect to find yourself renewed in body, soul, and mind and spirited into a new condition. But you do find, as I have, that a little here and a little there is evident in your experience. Compare the consciousness today with what it was four or six months ago. As I compare the results, I find it is a new result I am getting. I operate at a much higher law, and my consciousness even externalizes everything. Four or six months ago, it was a limited concept; it was a limited manifestation. There is a law of growth. We must learn to trust that law of growth; we must believe in it. If we will wait and know that divine law and order will bring that thing upon us (Ernest Holmes, *Science of Mind*)..Toni Stone once said, "It all matters. Thoughts 'spoken' and thoughts 'unspoken' they all register!"

The way you think, your attitudes, and your way about it all register in the realm of how things work out for you. Being cognizant of how you show up is an excellent remedy for discovering the source of your difficulties. The source of your problems is *you*. Well, now that that is settled, we know our jobs. Mary Baker Eddy said, "Thoughts unspoken are not unknown to the Divine Mind. "We are glad to know what the difficulty is so we can remedy the seeming problem" (Mary Baker Eddy, *Christ the Scientist*).

When Mary says "the seeming problem," that is where most people get stuck; they prefer to talk about the problem and own it instead of accepting that they are the problem. Their thinking is creating this experience operating with the Law of Growth.

It will continue to manifest until they wake up to a new way of thinking.

As Yes sang in the song "I've Seen All Good People," don't surround yourself with your "self."

Lead singer/lyricist Jon Anderson says that on the "Your Move" portion of this song, he was using the game of chess in this song as a metaphor for life's spiritual challenges. "Life is a game of strategically placed situations presented to you, and you have to learn to live with them and work with them," he said, "Doors are open, and sometimes they're closed. It's the idea that we are surrounded by a spirit or God or energy is in time with our understanding of who we are."

A few of the lyrics are below:

> I've seen all good people turn their heads each day so satisfied I'm on my way.
>
> I've seen all good people turn their heads each day so satisfied I'm on my way.
>
> Take a straight and stronger course to the corner of your life
>
> Don't surround yourself with yourself
>
> Don't surround yourself with yourself
>
> Move on back two squares
>
> Send an instant karma to me
>
> Initial it with loving care.

Ask, "What in this can I be grateful for?" How can I grow from this experience? What can I change in my thinking to change my circumstances?

Epilogue

Life is feedback. There is no place in a Universe where the Divine* is absent. Consciousness is always present at different levels, whether in a black hole, a star's birth, in dust, in water, or every life form, from the smallest only seen by microscope to the largest only seen by telescopes.

Humans can choose a level higher than all other life forms to operate from and don't come close to * "the everything and nothing" that I experienced during my near-death experience.

In his book, *The Order of Time,* Carlo Rovelli, wrote, "I have an enduring passion for Anaximander, the Greek philosopher who lived twenty-six centuries ago and understood that the earth floats in space, supported by nothing." We live in something we don't understand, and it's in plain sight. As we descend into lower-level thinking, influenced by the need to be right, we miss that doing the right thing is what is happening eternally in the Universe.

All creatures except for humans operate on instinct provided as necessary by creation. We have the choice of the level we use.

What if you are wrong? What if all humanity is wrong? I suggest that doing the right thing supersedes being right. Often I hear people say, "oh, this is just me, I cannot be anything but me."

Not true. Consider this, your brain is programmed much like a computer. Who programmed it? You have, over time. Negative people and events that you have responded to with anger, sadness, depression or any other emotion over time program your subconscious to respond in similar fashion when similar events occur. It's like driving. When you first got behind the wheel there was a lot to learn and remember. Now, what happens? It's automatic. I am sometimes driving and thinking, "who just drove for the past five miles," as I realize my mind was elsewhere.

As Joe Dispenza says, "you can re-mind yourself." Neuro specialists today call it pruning and sprouting. You can develop new neuro pathways as you observe yourself reacting in old familiar ways that no longer serve you. By self-observation you can prove this concept to yourself. I recommend the book, "Break the Habit of Being Yourself," by Joe Dispenza. I have spent over 25 years "re-minding" myself and proven it works for me. Don't take my word for it, try it.

It's a lifelong journey and you will find that you can quiet that incessant little voice and replace it with new neuro pathways that are positive and in alignment with the new person you envision.

In today's society, our leaders and most of the general population operate from being right, which is a lower level of consciousness. It's not much higher than instinct. When we react, we are stuck in instinct; when we respond, infinite possibilities open.

Here is a suggestion. Consider life as rides at the carnival or theme park. Some are wild and throw us around; some are happy, like floating merrily down a river. Have fun, and if you don't consider a superior intelligence behind life, perhaps you can think in terms of a teacher—whatever works for you.

I wish you well along this journey, and I wish everyone could get a peek at what's next as I did. We would not be so petty and small-minded.

My job is me, and that is a journey.

I am sorry for those of you I have offended, and today I can only offer this: "It seemed like a good idea at the time."

That thought helps me laugh at myself, and I am genuinely in awe of this gift called life.

Questions? Please e-mail me at steve@stevelentini.com

If you would like to attend one of my classes or receive coaching about overcoming your small-minded thinking, e-mail me as well. I am glad to help. It's my calling. ☺

DISCOVER YOUR LIFE'S PURPOSE!

Feel Like Your Just Drifting?

This Short Quiz Will Unlock
Unlock the Clarity You've Been Seeking

INPLAINSIGHT.PRO/BONUS

www.ingramcontent.com/pod-product-compliance
Lightning Source LLC
Chambersburg PA
CBHW031206090426
42736CB00009B/808